What's Wrong with the Circuit?

Fixing the Problem

Rosie McKee

D1712349

COMPUTER SCIENCE for the REAL World™

Rosen Classroom™

Published in 2018 by The Rosen Publishing Group, Inc.
29 East 21st Street, New York, NY 10010

Book Design: Jennifer Ryder-Talbot
Editor: Caitie McAneney

Photo Credits: Cover, p. 5, 11, 21 Sergey Novikov/Shutterstock.com; p. 6 Designua/
Shutterstock.com; p. 8-9, 18 haryigit/Shutterstock.com; p. 12 erashov/
Shutterstock.com; p. 14 Love Silhouette/Shutterstock.com; p. 15 Paolo De Gasperis/
Shutterstock.com; p. 16 mariva2017/Shutterstock.com.

Library of Congress Cataloging-in-Publication Data

Names: McKee, Rosie.
Title: What's wrong with the circuit?: fixing the problem / Rosie McKee.
Description: New York : Rosen Classroom, 2018. | Series: Computer Kids: Powered by
Computational Thinking | Includes glossary and index.
Identifiers: LCCN ISBN 9781508137603 (pbk.) | ISBN 9781538324462 (library bound) |
ISBN 9781538355558 (6 pack) | ISBN 9781538352823 (ebook)
Subjects: LCSH: Electric circuits--Juvenile literature. | Electric networks--Juvenile literature.
| Electricity--Juvenile literature.
Classification: LCC TK148.M35 2018 | DDC 621.319'2--dc23

Manufactured in the United States of America

CPSIA Compliance Information: Batch #WS18RC: For Further Information contact Rosen Publishing, New York, New York at 1-800-237-9932

Table of Contents

What Are Circuits?

We use electricity every single day. Electricity powers televisions, lights, laptops, and gaming systems. It is a kind of energy that's able to flow through **conductors**, like wires. Most metals are conductors, which means they allow energy to flow through them.

How does electricity make it to the device it has to power? Circuits are like electricity highways. They connect a power source to a device. Power sources include batteries, **solar cells**, and the electric grid. Power lines bring electricity from a source to your house. If you turn on a light switch in your house, it allows electricity to flow to the lights. Some circuits like this are large and **complex**, but simple circuits are easy to make!

You can buy a circuit kit with all the parts you need to make your own circuit.

Kinds of Circuits

Series Circuit   Parallel Circuit

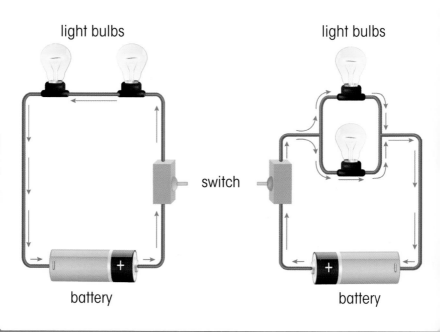

These pictures show the difference between series and parallel circuits.

Different Kinds of Circuits

Before building a circuit, make sure to learn about different kinds of circuits. There are two main kinds of circuits—series and parallel. Series circuits have a pathway along which the whole **current** flows through every single part. If multiple light bulbs are plugged in, the electricity has to flow through all of them. Parallel circuits divide the electricity between branches, with only part of the current flowing through each branch.

Christmas lights are good examples of the differences between series and parallel circuits. Some Christmas lights are series circuits. If one light bulb blows out, all of the lights turn off. Other lights are parallel circuits. If one light bulb blows out, the other lights will still have a current.

Circuit Parts

Before building a circuit, you will also have to learn about its different parts and what they do. Simple circuits have only a few parts for you to learn.

This series circuit has batteries, wires, a light bulb, and a switch.

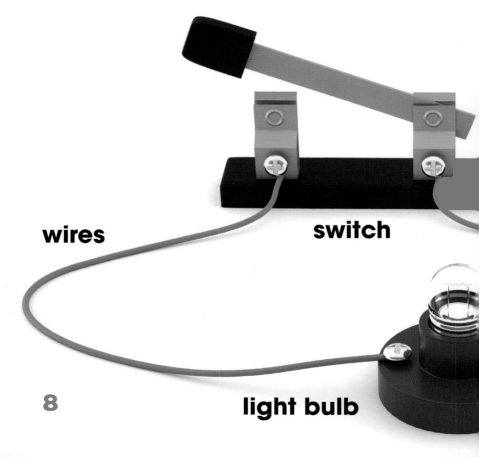

wires

switch

light bulb

The battery is the power source of the whole circuit. In order to transfer electricity from the battery to the light bulb, you must connect them with a wire. A switch is often placed in a circuit as a way for you to turn a light on and off. A wire must run from the light bulb to the switch. The most important part is completing the circuit so the electricity can flow. To do that, add a wire from the switch to the battery. Now you have a circular path for electricity!

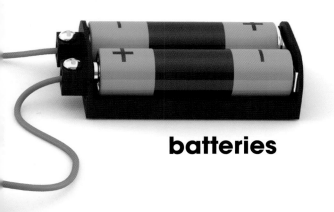

batteries

A Problem!

Whenever you build or make something, there is a chance that a problem may arise. The important thing is to never give up. Think about the situation clearly and take a step back to look at what might have gone wrong. Once you find the cause of a problem, then you will be able to figure out a solution. This is true for anything from circuits, to cooking, to coding. For example, computer programmers often have to find and fix problems in their code to make it work.

If you have a problem, it's important to stick with it until you find a solution.

Imagine you've built a circuit, but the light bulb won't light up. What went wrong? You can check each part of the circuit to see if it is the source of the problem.

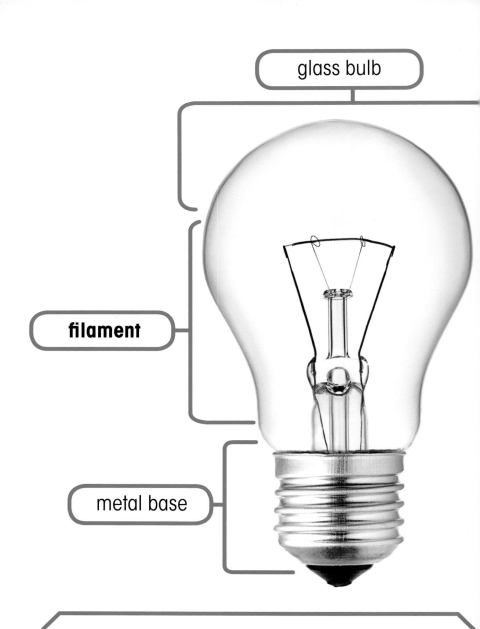

glass bulb

filament

metal base

This diagram shows the three basic parts to a light bulb.

Checking the Bulb

Could the light bulb be the source of the problem? Let's learn more about light bulbs to find out.

There are three basic parts to every light bulb. There is a metal base. Metal is a conductor, so this base allows electricity to travel through it. The base is connected to a thin, metal wire called a filament. A glass bulb surrounds the filament to keep air away from it. Electricity flows from the base to the filament, which is made of a metal that heats up and begins to glow. You can check the bulb to make sure there's nothing wrong with any of the parts. Is the filament in place? Is the glass cracked?

Checking the Wires

Wires allow electricity to flow from one object in the circuit to the other. Because of this, wires have to be great conductors. They are usually made from copper. Copper is a metal that is light orange in color. Copper wire is covered in a **material** that acts as an **insulator**. That keeps you from getting a shock when you touch the wires.

The wires in a circuit kit usually have little clips on the ends of them. They are called alligator clips because they resemble an alligator's jaws. The clips allow you to clamp on to each object easily. When you check your wires, make sure all of the clips are connected to the objects in the correct way.

alligator clips

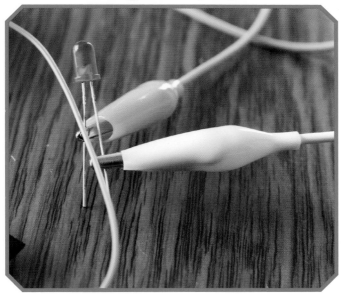

Wires must be conductors in order to work.

One side of the battery is positive and one side is negative.

Checking the Battery

The battery is the power source for the circuit. Maybe the problem has to do with the battery. What are batteries, anyway? Batteries are **containers** for energy. They store energy in the form of chemicals until it is needed. When you use a battery, chemical energy is **transformed** into electrical energy.

You may already know that a battery has a positive side and a negative side. The positive side is called the cathode, and it has a bump on it. The negative side is called the anode. Batteries work when there is an electrical difference between the two sides. If a battery is dead, **chemical reactions** won't happen. Check your battery in another device to see if it still works!

Checking the Switch

So far, there have been no issues with any of the parts of the circuit. There's still one part left to check—the switch. The switch controls the flow of electricity through the circuit. It is an "on/off" switch, like a light switch on the wall in your home.

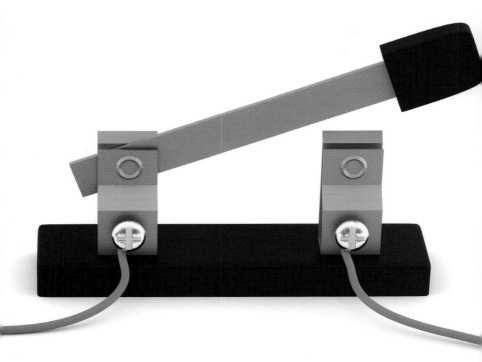

When the switch is closed, the path of electricity is complete. That will turn the light on. When the switch is open, it breaks the path of electricity. That means that the electricity can no longer make it from the battery to the light bulb and back. Switches in circuit kits often have an arm that is in an open position or a closed position. Do you think the problem has to do with your circuit's switch?

This switch is open. The arm is up.

Finding the Problem

So far, you have checked the light bulbs, battery, and wires. Now, you're checking the switch. Is the arm of the switch down, making it a closed pathway for electricity?

Imagine that the arm is up. That is the problem! Because the arm of the switch is up, the path of electricity is **disrupted**. The electricity can't make it from the power source to the light bulb. It's very important to find the problem when something doesn't work. Then, you can examine the problem and decide what might work as a solution. What do you know about switches that could help you solve this problem?

Once you find the problem, you can **implement** a solution!

A Solution!

Can you think of a solution to this problem? By learning about each part in the circuit, you now understand how they all work together to make a light bulb light up. You already know that when a switch is closed, the electricity can flow. If the problem is that the arm of the switch is lifted and the switch is open, then the solution is to drop the arm and close the switch.

Try this solution. Did it work? Testing a solution is very important when you're trying to fix something. Imagine that your light bulb now lights up. You have successfully found and fixed a problem, and you learned about electricity along the way!

Glossary

chemical reaction: A chemical change that happens when two or more things combine to form a new thing.

complex: Having to do with many parts that work together.

conductor: Matter through which electricity flows easily.

container: An object used to hold something.

current: A flow of electricity resulting from the movement of particles such as electrons.

disrupt: To interrupt the normal course of something.

filament: A threadlike object, often made of metal.

implement: To carry out.

insulator: A material that prevents the transfer of electricity.

material: Something from which something else can be made.

solar cell: A cell that changes sunlight into electricity and is used as a power source.

transform: To change into something else.

Index